Ghillie Başan has written over 40 books on different culinary cultures and has been nominated for the Glenfiddich Award, the Guild of Food Writers Award and the Cordon Bleu World Food Media Award. Her food and travel articles have appeared in a huge variety of newspapers and magazines, including *The Sunday Times*, *The Daily Telegraph*, *BBC Good Food* magazine and *Eating* magazine. As a broadcaster she has presented and contributed to many BBC radio programmes. As well as running cookery workshops, she also works as a flavour and food pairing consultant for bar tenders and chefs.

# The *Scottish Brunch* Bible

Ghillie Başan

Illustrated by Bob Dewar

BIRLINN

First published in 2021 by
Birlinn Limited
West Newington House
10 Newington Road Edinburgh
EH9 1QS

*www.birlinn.co.uk*

Copyright © Ghillie Başan 2021

Artwork copyright © Bob Dewar 2021

ISBN: 978 1 78027 662 5

British Library Cataloguing-in-Publication Data
A catalogue record for this book is available from
the British Library

Designed and typeset by Mark Blackadder

Printed and bound by Bell & Bain Ltd, Glasgow

# Contents

## Brunch with Eggs

Fresh oysters, dressed crab, smoked      34
    Gigha halibut and spicy deep-fried eggs

Herring in oatmeal with creamy scrambled eggs   36

Forager's frittata      38

Hot-smoked salmon huevos rancheros     40

Fried eggs and chanterelles on polenta wedges   42

Portobello mushroom burgers with mozzarella,   45
    bacon, tomato and fried eggs

Duck eggs with fried lettuce, wild herbs     47
    and chilli oil

Wild garlic shakshuka with yogurt     49

## Brunch on Bread

Hot croissants with bacon, Cheddar,     52
    avocado and mayonnaise

Cheesy French toast with garlicky rosemary   54
    mushrooms

Pancetta scallops with Caesar salad bruschetta   57

Orkney marinated herring with granola     59
    Waldorf salad on rye bread

## Baked Potato Brunch

Baked potato with smoked salmon and     63
    chilli scrambled eggs

Baked potato with lemon lovage tuna salad   65

Baked potato with haggis and     67
    marmalade chipolatas

# Introduction

The first time I realised that brunch was more than a mid-morning fry-up after a late night out and the inevitable lazy lie in was when I was invited to a 'Brunch Meeting' – a business meeting in a hotel with a breakfast-style buffet that included noodle dishes, spicy eggs, pancakes and rice pudding. That was some thirty years ago. Since then I have noticed the rising popularity of brunch at symposiums, on travel itineraries and 'Champagne Brunch' birthday parties and weddings – the bigger the event, the more creative the brunch. As morning merges with midday and food trends creep into our kitchens, brunch seems to have become a versatile platform for showcasing different traditions and fashionable dishes, embracing what is often the street food of different culinary cultures. In Scotland, we might find familiar egg dishes, potato scones and pancakes on the nation's menus but we are just as likely to come across Nasi Goreng in Glasgow, Shakshuka on Skye and Masala Beans in Aberdeen.

On days when time is more generous and food is not rushed, brunch should evoke pleasure and relaxation and, perhaps, an opportunity to try something new. It is the epitome of sociable eating. So, this Brunch Bible is by no means a reflection of Scottish tradition, but more of a representation of how our tastes and cooking have developed, combining local produce with global inspiration.

By definition, the word 'brunch' is a 'portmanteau' of breakfast and lunch and is regularly served with some form of alcoholic drink, like champagne or a cocktail, any time before 3pm! The concept is thought to have originated in Britain in 1895 when the writer Guy Beringer wrote an article describing brunch as a meal for 'Saturday-night carousers'. Suggesting it as a 'cheerful, social and inciting' alternative to an early Sunday dinner he wrote: 'It puts you in a good temper; it makes you satisfied with yourself and your fellow beings. It sweeps away the worries and cobwebs of the week.'

With such a description, it's not surprising that 'brunch' became established in metropolitan Britain, and in places like the United States and Australia. It seems to have started out as a Sunday tradition and often combined typical British breakfast fare, such as fried eggs and bacon, with sweet pancakes and puddings in a relaxed help-yourself style. And now that it has become a trend and not reserved for Sundays alone, there are brunch venues everywhere you go – pop-up and static – offering the requisite mix of relaxed eating and sociability with culinary twists on tradition combined with spices and sauces, adapting dishes to suit the theme. So, on a morning when breakfast time has passed and lunch is still on the horizon, a good brunch can become the focus of the day – until 3 p.m., it seems, if we follow its definition!

As the words 'flexible' and 'sociable' form the foundations of brunch, we can strive less for top-chef perfection and focus more on one-pan concoctions packed with flavour. Traditional peasant fare like soupy stews, savoury porridge, spicy tortillas and sizzling omelettes are common late-morning street-stall snacks in other parts of the world and can be easily adapted to brunch in Scotland. Throw snobbery and traditions into the wind and open your cupboards and fridges to bring out the sauce, the chutney and the pickles, whatever suits your mood. Add salads and toppings to make your brunch zing or crunch and play with texture, tart or sweet. Eat from the pot or pan, serve the dish on a board not a plate – save yourself some washing up – enjoy it outside if you can and, if you want an accompanying alcoholic drink, be inventive with cocktails and spirits; don't try to pair the dish with wine. Combine sweet with savoury, eat with your fingers and let the juices dribble down your chin. There simply are no rules for a good brunch – it can be as simple and traditional, complex and international, or as boozy as you wish.

# Brunch Accessories

Little mouthfuls of fresh, piquant, crunchy or
creamy salads, salsas and sauces just add that extra
splash of colour and flavour dimension to a
brunch dish, often lifting a simple combination to
a new level. So, here are some suggestions that
could dress up many of the dishes in this little
book – it's really a case of mixing and matching
to your own taste.

# Bloody Mary salad

**Serves 2**

1 red onion, finely chopped
1–2 tablespoons vodka
A selection of small, sweet tomatoes, quartered
2–3 celery stalks and leaves, chopped
1 tablespoon chopped green olives
2 tablespoons white wine vinegar
2 teaspoons creamed horseradish
1 tablespoon Worcestershire sauce
1 teaspoon Tabasco
2 tablespoons olive oil
Sea salt and freshly ground black pepper

In a bowl, mix the onion with the vodka and leave to sit for 10 minutes. Add the tomatoes, celery and olives. Whisk the vinegar with the horseradish, Worcestershire sauce, Tabasco and slowly add the olive oil. Season with salt and pepper and pour the dressing over the salad. Don't toss until you serve.

# Guacamole salsa

**Serves 3–4**

2 large tomatoes
1 red onion, finely chopped
2 avocados, skinned, stoned and diced
1–2 green chillies, deseeded and finely chopped
2 garlic cloves, crushed
A bunch of fresh coriander, finely chopped
Juice of 2 limes
Sea salt and freshly ground black pepper

Bring a small pan of water to the boil. Drop in the tomatoes for 20–30 seconds, then drain and refresh under cold water. This helps to separate the flesh from the skin, which you can pull off with your fingers. Halve the tomatoes, scrape out the seeds, and dice the flesh.

Tip the tomatoes into a bowl with the onions, avocados, and chillies. Combine the lime juice with the crushed garlic and coriander, season with salt and pepper and pour it over the salad. Toss well.

# Gazpacho salad

**Serves 2–3**

**For the dressing:**
3–4 garlic cloves
½ teaspoon sea salt
1 teaspoon cumin seeds
1 teaspoon coriander seeds
4 tablespoons olive oil
1 tablespoon vinegar
Juice of 1 lemon
2 teaspoons honey
Freshly ground black pepper

**For the salad:**
1–2 tablespoons olive oil
2 slices day-old bread, broken into small pieces
A handful of cherry or sugardrop tomatoes, halved
A chunk of cucumber, deseeded and finely diced
1 yellow or orange pepper, deseeded and finely diced
1 small red onion, finely chopped
1 fresh green or red chilli, deseeded and finely sliced
A small bunch flat-leaf parsley, finely chopped
    (reserve a little for garnishing)

For the dressing, use a mortar and pestle to crush the
garlic to a paste with a little of the salt, cumin and
coriander seeds. Add the oil, vinegar, lemon juice and

honey and season with a good grinding of pepper and the rest of the salt.

For the salad, heat enough olive oil to cover the base of a frying pan. Toss in the bread chunks and fry until crispy and golden brown. Drain on kitchen paper. In a bowl, combine the tomatoes, cucumber, pepper, onion and chilli with most of the parsley.

Assemble the salad by layering the fried bread with the chopped vegetables, finishing with bread and the reserved parsley at the top. Drizzle the dressing over everything but don't toss – you want some of the bread to remain crispy and the flavours will mingle when you serve.

# Tartare potatoes

**Serves 3–4**

450g (1lb) waxy salad or new potatoes
1 tablespoon olive oil
1 tablespoon white wine vinegar or cider vinegar
1 teaspoon Dijon mustard
2 tablespoons soured cream
Sea salt and freshly ground black pepper
1–2 shallots, finely chopped
1 tablespoon capers in vinegar, drained
Roughly 6–8 small gherkins, finely chopped
A small bunch of chives, parsley and dill, all finely chopped together

First make the tartare dressing. Combine the oil with the vinegar, mustard and soured cream and season to taste.

Boil the potatoes in water until tender, but still have a bite to them. Drain and break, or roughly cut, into small chunks and toss in the dressing and shallots while still warm, making sure you coat the potatoes. Toss in the capers, gherkins and fresh herbs.

# Tangy pickles

**Serves 3–4**

1 large carrot, julienned
1 white turnip, julienned
½ a cucumber, peeled, deseeded and julienned
2 shallots, finely sliced
1 red bird's-eye chilli, halved and deseeded
4 tablespoons rice vinegar
2 tablespoons granulated sugar
1 teaspoon salt
Sesame seeds

Place the carrot, turnip and cucumber in a bowl and add the other ingredients. Mix well and leave to sit for at least 1 hour. You can make these ahead of time and keep in a jar in the fridge for 1–2 weeks.

# Garlic mayonnaise

**Makes approximately 400g (14oz)**
2 cloves garlic
½ teaspoon sea salt
2 large free-range egg yolks
Freshly ground black pepper
250ml (9fl oz) fruity extra virgin olive oil
½ a lemon

Mash the garlic to a paste with half a teaspoon of salt,
using a mortar and pestle. Stir in the yolks with a
grinding of black pepper. Add the olive oil, drop by drop
and then quickening to a trickle, whisking all the time,
until you have a light mayonnaise that stands in peaks.
Season with a squeeze of lemon.

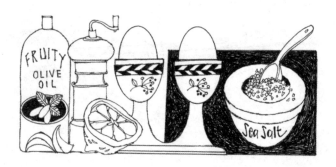

# Marie Rose sauce

**Makes approximately 250g (9oz)**

200g (7oz) mayonnaise
2 tablespoons tomato ketchup
1 teaspoon Worcestershire sauce
1–2 drops Tabasco
Sherry or brandy to taste
Juice of ½ a lemon
Sea salt and freshly ground black pepper

Combine the mayonnaise, tomato ketchup,
Worcestershire sauce and Tabasco in a bowl. Stir in
enough brandy to taste, and season with the lemon, salt
and pepper. This can be kept chilled.

# Avocado cream

---

**Serves 2–4**

2 avocados
2 tablespoons crème fraîche
Juice of 1 lime
1 garlic clove, crushed
Sea salt and freshly ground black pepper

---

Mash the avocado, or puree in a blender, and beat in the crème fraîche, lime juice and garlic. Season to taste with salt and pepper. If you are making this cream ahead of time, put the avocado stones into the bowl with the mixture to keep it from turning brown in colour, but remove them before serving.

# Brunch in a Bowl

# Bloody Mary shellfish stew

If you're a fan of Bloody Marys for brunch, you can't go wrong with this fiery stew. Packed with fresh Scottish seafood, chillies, tomatoes and a splash of vodka, Worcestershire sauce and Tabasco, it's either a pick-me-up or a back-to-bed sort of brunch.

---

**Serves 4**

2 tablespoons olive oil
2 onions, finely chopped
3–4 garlic cloves, finely chopped
2 teaspoons dried chilli flakes
2 x 400g (14oz) tins of plum tomatoes
2 teaspoons granulated sugar
1 red pepper, deseeded and chopped
600ml (1 pint) fish or chicken stock
300ml (½ pint) vodka
Sea salt and freshly ground black pepper
Roughly 500g (1lb 2oz) mixed fresh, prepared shellfish
A bunch of fresh coriander, finely chopped

**For serving:**
Worcestershire sauce
Tabasco
Vodka

---

Heat 1 tablespoon of oil in a heavy-based pot or wok and fry half the onions and garlic until soft. Add the chilli flakes and 1 can of tomatoes with 1 teaspoon of sugar and cook to a thick pulp. Tip the pulp into a blender and whiz until smooth.

Heat the remaining tablespoon of oil in a heavy-based pot or wok and stir in the rest of the onion with the chopped pepper for 2–3 minutes. Add the second can of plum tomatoes with the rest of the sugar and pour in the stock and vodka. Bring the liquid to the boil, then turn down the heat and simmer for about 30 minutes.

Stir in the whizzed sauce, bring the liquid back to the boil and season to taste. Add in half the coriander and then add in the shellfish for 1–2 minutes to just warm through.

Ladle the thick stew into bowls, garnish with the rest of the coriander and serve with chunks of crusty bread to dunk into it. Pass around the Worcestershire sauce, Tabasco and vodka to splash into the stew.

# Smoky bacon and black pudding with hot hummus

I have been writing about hot hummus for over 30 years and I never tire of it as it is one of my favourite dishes for any time of day! I first came across it in a small village in eastern Anatolia where I was given it for supper and for breakfast with a chunk of bread but it is also traditionally served with grilled meat, or with thin strips of cured air-dried beef, which made me think it would make a great brunch dish with smoked bacon and black pudding. And it does!

---

**Serves 2–4**

2 x 400g (14oz) tins of chickpeas, drained and thoroughly rinsed
2 teaspoons cumin seeds
2–3 cloves garlic, crushed
Roughly 4 tablespoons olive oil
Juice of 2 lemons
2 tablespoons tahini
6 tablespoons thick, creamy yogurt
Sea salt and freshly ground black pepper
4–8 rashers of smoked, streaky bacon
A knob of butter
2–4 slices black pudding

---

Preheat the oven to 200°C (180°C fan), 400°F, Gas 6. Hummus is much easier to make using an electric blender and you can get a smoother consistency than pounding it by hand. So, whiz together the chickpeas, cumin seeds, garlic, olive oil, and lemon to a thick paste. Add the tahini and continue to whiz until the mixture is really thick and smooth. Add the yogurt and whiz until the mixture has loosened a little and the texture is creamy. Season generously with salt and pepper and tip the mixture into individual ovenproof dishes, or a single one.

Cut the bacon rashers into 3 or 4 pieces and, using the blade of a knife, stretch them out so that they become thinner. Place the bacon pieces over the top of the hummus so it is covered and pop it in the oven for about 20 minutes, or until the bacon is lightly browned and crisp.

Meanwhile, heat the butter in a pan and fry the black pudding slices for 2–3 minutes until slightly crisp. Drain on kitchen paper and keep warm.

When the hummus is ready, serve it in the individual oven dishes, or spoon it into bowls. Crumble the black pudding over the top and enjoy with chunks of crusty bread and a simple salad.

# Honey-mustard sausages with sweet potato mash

Sweet potatoes, yams and a variety of gourds can be roasted, boiled or steamed to make a thick nourishing porridge or a buttery mash. To get all of the natural sweetness and vitamins from the sweet potatoes, I like to bake them in foil to soften the skins and then mash the flesh and skin together. For the sausages, mustard and honey, all three are usually available in a good butcher where you will probably have a choice of plain and flavored sausages as well as local honey and a grain mustard with whisky.

---

**Serves 2**

Roughly 4–5 small sweet potatoes, scrubbed clean
Butter or olive oil, for mashing
Sea salt and black pepper
Juice of 1 orange
A small bunch parsley, finely chopped
450g (1lb) top-quality pork, beef or venison sausages, or chipolatas
Sunflower oil
2 tablespoons honey
2 tablespoons grain mustard

---

Preheat the oven to 200°C (180°C fan), 400°F, Gas 6. Wrap the sweet potatoes in foil, pop them on a baking tray and bake them in the oven until soft – this will take at least 1 hour, depending on the size of the potatoes.

Line a baking tray with greaseproof paper and, using a piece of kitchen paper, smear it with a little sunflower oil. Line up the sausages in rows. Mix together the honey and grain mustard and smear it over the top of the sausages. Pop them in the oven for about 30 minutes, turning them once so that they are coated and browned evenly. Once cooked, brown and sticky, keep the sausages warm.

When the potatoes are soft, remove the foil and place them in a bowl. Mash them with a little butter or olive oil, beat in the orange juice and parsley, and season with salt and pepper.

Assemble the mashed sweet potato in bowls, pile on the sausages and serve with eggs or salad.

# Kale ribollita with Dunlop Bonnet

Ribollita is a traditional Italian peasant dish, designed to use up bits of stale loaf and to be eaten on its own as a hearty mid-morning snack or evening meal. Simple and cheap to make, it is ideal for a Scottish brunch using seasonal kale, cabbage or chard and any leftover bread you have. You can toast slices of bread, rub them with garlic, drizzle in olive oil and place them in the base of each bowl before ladling the body of the soup over them; you can layer the bread through the soup or simply add chunks at the end to stir in. It is all very flexible and delicious, served with a generous grating of Dunlop Bonnet, a deliciously tangy goat's cheese from Ayrshire, or a similar hard cheese like Parmesan, and can be topped with a poached egg if you like.

---

**Serves 4**

2–3 tablespoons olive oil
1 onion, finely chopped
1 large carrot, peeled and diced
2 good-sized potatoes, peeled and diced
1 celery stick, diced
4–6 garlic cloves, finely chopped
A few sprigs of rosemary and sage, finely chopped
1 teaspoon cumin seeds
1 teaspoon fennel seeds
2 x 400g (14oz) tins chopped tomatoes

1 teaspoon granulated sugar
1–2 teaspoons dried chilli flakes
900ml (1½ pints) chicken or vegetable stock
300ml (½ pint) red wine
Roughly 250g (9oz) fresh kale, cabbage or chard leaves
1 x 400g (14oz) tin of cannellini beans, drained and rinsed
Sea salt and freshly ground black pepper
Roughly 4 thick slices stale or toasted bread – ciabatta, baguette,
    country loaf, sourdough – broken into chunks
150g (5½oz) Dunlop Bonnet, or other hard, tangy cheese, grated
Olive oil to drizzle
A small bunch of fresh parsley, finely chopped

———————————

Heat the oil in a large, heavy-based saucepan and stir in
the onion, carrot, potatoes, celery, garlic, rosemary and
sage with the cumin and fennel. Stirring from time to
time, sauté the mixture for about 20 minutes, until
reduced and fragrant. Add the tomatoes with the sugar
and chilli and cook the mixture for another 20–25
minutes until it is thick and saucy. This gives you a richly
flavoured base for the stock.

Pour in the stock and wine and bring to the boil.
Add the kale and cook for about 10 minutes. Add the
beans and cook for another 10 minutes. Season to taste
with salt and pepper.

Toss in the bread with half of the cheese. Ladle the
thick soup into bowls, drizzle with olive oil and garnish
with parsley and the rest of the grated cheese.

# Smoky quinoa and sweetcorn porridge

Originally an ancient seed from the Andes, quinoa has become a familiar fixture on the salad menus of Scotland's vegetarian and vegan cafés, partly because it is cheap and packed with protein. Simmered into porridge, the seeds retain a satisfying fluffy grittiness and, combined with fresh Guacamole salsa (p. 13) and a dollop of soured cream, you can create a nutritious brunch bowl.

---

**Serves 2–3**

1 tablespoon olive oil and knob of butter
1 teaspoon cumin seeds
1 teaspoon caraway seeds
2 teaspoons fennel seeds
1 onion, finely chopped
2 teaspoons dried chilli flakes
150g (5½oz) quinoa, rinsed and drained
600ml (1 pint) chicken or vegetable stock
1 x 325g (11oz) tin of sweetcorn in water, rinsed and drained
2 teaspoons smoked paprika
200g (7oz) aged goat's or ewe's cheese or other hard, tangy cheese, grated
A small bunch fresh flat-leaf parsley and mint, finely chopped together (reserve a little for garnishing)
Sea salt and freshly ground black pepper

**For serving:**
Guacamole salsa
Soured cream
Extra chilli

———————————

Heat the oil with the butter in a heavy-based pot. Stir in the cumin, caraway and fennel seeds for 1–2 minutes, until fragrant. Add the onion and, when it begins to colour, stir in the chilli flakes with the quinoa, coating it in the spices. Pour in the stock, bring it to the boil, turn down the heat and simmer for about 15 minutes.

When the porridge begins to thicken, toss in the sweetcorn and smoked paprika and simmer for a further 10 minutes. Gradually, beat in the cheese – add a little more stock or water if you think the quinoa needs it – and stir in most of the parsley and mint.

Season to taste – add more smoked paprika or chilli if you like – and spoon the hot porridge into bowls. Top with guacamole salsa and a dollop of soured cream and garnish with the reserved mint and parsley.

# Brunch with Eggs

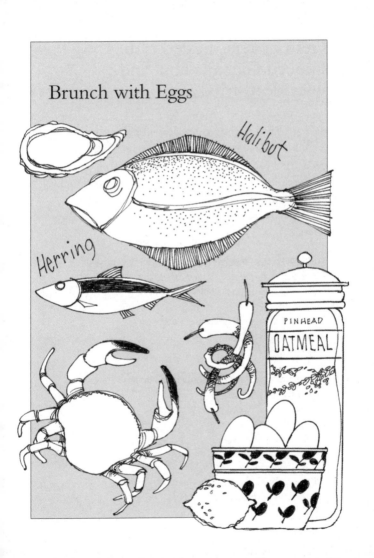

# Fresh oysters, dressed crab, smoked Gigha halibut and spicy deep-fried eggs

As Scotland is notorious for deep-frying everything including Mars Bars, I couldn't resist including these deep-fried eggs as a complete contrast to the elegance and freshness of our quality seafood. A bit of a tongue-in-cheek brunch!

---

**Serves 2**

4–8 fresh oysters, shucked (your fishmonger can do this)
2 dressed crabs (your fishmonger can do this)
6 slices smoked Gigha halibut
1–2 lemons, halved
A small bunch of parsley, finely chopped
Black pepper, for grinding
Tabasco (optional)

A finger-sized piece of ginger, peeled and roughly chopped
2 garlic cloves, chopped
1–2 red chillies, deseeded and chopped
1 tablespoon sesame oil
1 teaspoon cumin seeds
1 teaspoon fennel seeds
1–2 teaspoons honey
200g (7oz) baby plum or cherry tomatoes, halved
1 avocado, skinned, stoned and diced

Sunflower or vegetable oil, for deep-frying
4 eggs
A small bunch of coriander, finely chopped

---

Arrange the oysters in their bottom shells around the edge of a large board with the smoked halibut and dressed crab, and lemon halves for squeezing. Scatter a little parsley over them and season with black pepper and a drop of Tabasco, if you like.

Using a mortar and pestle, pound the ginger, garlic and chillies to a paste. Heat the sesame oil in a heavy-based pan and stir in the cumin and fennel seeds until fragrant. Add the paste and cook for a minute, then stir in the honey. Toss in the tomatoes and cook until they crinkle. Toss in the avocado, season with salt and take off the heat.

Heat enough sunflower oil in a wok to deep-fry. Break an egg into a ladle and slip it into the oil. Do the same with the rest of the eggs and fry until crispy and blistered.

Lift them out of the oil with a slotted spoon, drain on kitchen paper, and slip them into the spicy tomatoes. Garnish with the coriander and place the pan in the middle of board amongst the elegant shells and golden-fringed halibut.

# Herring in oatmeal with creamy scrambled eggs

This was my mother's favourite brunch. Herring, or 'silver darlings' as we know them in Scotland, were her favourite fish – soused, pickled, stuffed, baked or fried in oatmeal, which was the traditional way of cooking them when she was a child. To complete your brunch plate, you might like to serve Tartare potatoes (p. 16) with the herring.

---

**Serves 2**

**For the herring:**
2 eggs
60ml (2fl oz) milk
30g (1oz) plain flour
100g (3½oz) porridge oats or fine oatmeal
2 herring, boned, gutted and butterflied (your fishmonger
    will do this for you)
Sunflower oil
Sea salt and freshly ground black pepper
1 lemon, halved or quartered

**For the eggs:**
6–8 eggs
150ml (5fl oz) double cream
A small handful parsley, finely chopped
Freshly ground black pepper
A generous knob of butter

---

To prepare the herring, beat the eggs with the milk in a shallow bowl and tip the flour and oatmeal into two separate shallow bowls. Pat the herring dry and season well with salt and pepper. Dip each butterflied herring into the flour first to coat it, then into the egg and milk, and finally into the oatmeal. Make sure you press the oatmeal onto the herring.

Heat the oil in a wide frying pan and place the herring in skin-side down. Fry for 2 minutes, then turn them over for another 2 minutes, until golden and crispy. Keep warm while you scramble the eggs.

In a bowl, quickly whisk the eggs and cream together with the parsley, and season well with salt and pepper. Begin to melt the butter in a non-stick frying pan, swirling it so that the butter spreads evenly, and just before it has fully melted tip in the egg mixture. As the eggs begin to cook around the edges, draw them into the centre with a spatula, so that you create curds but don't stir them vigorously.

While they are still a little underdone, divide the scrambled eggs onto plates and place the herring beside them. Serve with the lemon to squeeze over the herring and tartare potatoes or a salad of your choice.

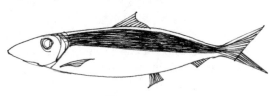

# Forager's frittata

This brunch go-to is based on Kuku Sabzi, the classic green Persian frittata which is flipped over so that the cooked browned bottom becomes the top. If you have kale, beet leaves, borage or chard and any other aromatic leaves, such as wild garlic, sorrel, lovage, sweet cicely, spignel and hedge garlic, just add them to the mix.

---

**Serves 4–6**

500g (1lb 2oz) fresh spinach leaves, washed and drained
300g (10oz) fresh kale or beet leaves, washed and drained
1 leek, trimmed and sliced
60g (2oz) butter
2 garlic cloves, finely chopped
2 teaspoons caraway or lovage seeds
2 large handfuls of wild aromatic leaves, roughly chopped,
      or a combination of mint, basil and coriander
10 large eggs
Sea salt and fresh pepper
A little olive oil

---

Preheat the oven to 180°C (160°C fan), 350°F, Gas 4. First, steam all the fresh leaves, until soft. Squeeze out the excess water and roughly chop.

Heat half the butter in a pan and stir in the garlic and caraway seeds for a minute. Toss in the leeks and cook over a low heat until soft and lightly browned.

Tip the leeks into a bowl. Add the chopped steamed leaves along with all the aromatic ones. Crack the eggs into the bowl, season with salt and pepper, and mix everything together well.

Heat the rest of the butter with a little olive oil in a non-stick, ovenproof frying pan, using a piece of kitchen paper to spread it over the base and up the sides. Pour in the egg mixture and cook over a low heat for about 10 minutes, until the frittata begins to set and the bottom is golden brown (use a spatula to lift the edge to check). Pop the pan in the oven and cook for about 15 minutes until firm to touch and lightly browned on top.

Run a thin spatula around the edge of the frittata to make sure it isn't sticking to the sides of the pan. Place a flat baking sheet or light wooden board over the pan and flip the frittata upside down. Serve hot and add grilled bacon, sausages, or a salad to your plate, if you like.

Borage

Sorrel

# Hot-smoked salmon huevos rancheros

To my mind, hot-smoked salmon should be almost sweet and juicy, not salty and dry. In fact, it should be so moist it almost melts in your mouth. Curing with honey and smoking it over whisky staves adds to the flavour and velvety texture, which can be enhanced by adding the crunch of samphire grass or spring onions – perfect for padding out the Mexican brunch classic, huevos rancheros.

---

**Serves 2**

**For the salsa:**
1 tablespoon olive, peanut or corn oil with a knob of butter
1 onion, finely chopped
4 garlic cloves, finely chopped
1 teaspoon cumin seeds
Roughly 8 preserved anchovies, drained of oil
1–2 fresh red or green chillies, deseeded and finely chopped
1–2 teaspoons granulated sugar
1 x 400g (14oz) tin of plum tomatoes
Sea salt and freshly ground black pepper

A knob of butter
2–4 eggs
2–4 corn tortillas
250g (9oz) hot-smoked salmon, broken up into chunks

A handful of fresh samphire grass, snapped into pieces, or spring
    onions, finely sliced
A small bunch of fresh coriander, coarsely chopped

---

Heat the oil and butter in a small pan and toss in the
onion, garlic and cumin seeds. Cook for 1–2 minutes
until soft. Stir in the anchovy fillets, until they melt into
the oil. Add the fresh chillies, sugar and tomatoes and
cook for about 20 minutes, breaking the tomatoes up,
until you have a thick sauce. Season well to taste. Keep
warm.

Melt the butter in a pan and fry the eggs just how
you like them. Warm the tortillas in a flat pan, on a
girdle, in the oven or microwave and lay them on plates.
Spoon some of the salsa on to each tortilla, scatter the
salmon and samphire grass over the sauce and place the
eggs on top. Finish with a dollop of sauce and garnish
with the fresh coriander.

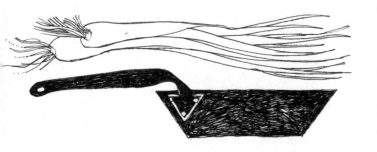

# Fried eggs and chanterelles on polenta wedges

This brunch dish is a tasty way to showcase pretty orange chanterelles and their delicate apricot flavour when in season, but you could easily substitute them with other wild mushrooms such as porcini or birch boletus, or with shop-bought chestnut mushrooms.

---

**Serves 4**

**For the polenta:**
400ml (14fl oz) milk
400ml (14fl oz) water
A few black peppercorns
1 small onion, halved
A sprig of thyme
150g (5oz) quick-cook polenta
30g (1oz) butter
Sea salt
Freshly ground black pepper
2 tablespoons olive oil, for frying

**For the chanterelles and eggs:**
1–2 tablespoons olive or rapeseed oil
1 plump clove of garlic, finely chopped
2–3 handfuls fresh chanterelles, or other wild or cultivated
      mushrooms
½ a lemon
Sea salt

Freshly ground black pepper
4 eggs

**For serving:**
Fresh thyme leaves
Parmesan shavings
1 lemon, cut into quarters, for squeezing

---

First prepare the polenta. Pour the milk and water into a saucepan, add the peppercorns, onion and thyme and bring to scalding point. Turn off the heat and leave to infuse for 20 minutes.

Strain the infused liquid into a clean saucepan and bring it back to scalding point. Reduce the heat to simmer and add the polenta in a thin stream, stirring all the time until smooth. Simmer gently for 4–5 minutes then remove it from the heat. Beat in the butter, season well and tip the polenta onto a cool surface – a marble slab or a wide dish or plate – and smooth it into an even disc or rectangle and leave to cool. When cold cut the polenta into 4 wedges or thick fingers.

Heat the olive oil in a pan and fry the polenta wedges for 2–3 minutes on each side until they form a golden-brown crust. Keep warm while you fry the mushrooms and eggs.

Drizzle a little oil into a pan and toss in the garlic until it begins to colour. Toss in the chanterelles and sauté over a medium to high heat, tipping the pan if there is too much water seeping from the fungi, and keep tossing

until the pan is almost dry and the chanterelles are lightly browned. Add a squeeze of lemon juice and season with salt and pepper. Keep warm.

Drizzle some more oil into a pan and fry the eggs how you like them. Place each polenta wedge on a plate, top each one with a fried egg and spoon the chanterelles over them. Garnish with the thyme leaves and Parmesan shavings and serve with the lemon wedges.

# Portobello mushroom burgers with mozzarella, bacon, tomato and fried eggs

Portobello mushrooms are great to bake or grill and, although they seep water on cooking and reduce in size, you can still stuff them or pile ingredients on top. My children used to enjoy making burgers with them, often by stuffing a fried egg in between two baked mushrooms or by layering up mozzarella and tomato on top.

**Serves 2**

4 portobello mushrooms
Olive oil
4 rashers of streaky bacon
2 slices mozzarella
2 slices tomato
4–8 basil leaves
2 eggs

Preheat the oven to 200°C (180°C fan) 400°F, Gas 6. Twist off the stalks and place the mushrooms top-side down in an oven dish – you can add the stalks to the dish too. Drizzle a little oil over the mushrooms and pop them in the oven for 20 minutes.

Meanwhile, fry or grill the bacon rashers until golden but not too crispy.

Take the mushrooms out of the oven and drain off any liquid. Place a piece of sliced mozzarella onto two of them – sit them inside the shell if possible. Add a slice of tomato on top, followed by a few basil leaves and the bacon. Cap with the remaining two mushrooms to form burgers. Apply a little pressure to keep everything in place then return the mushrooms to the oven for 5–6 minutes, until the mozzarella has melted.

Meanwhile, heat a little oil in the pan and fry the eggs how you like them. When it comes to serving, you can lift the top mushroom and place the egg underneath, or you can serve the egg alongside the mushroom burger. Add ketchup, brown sauce, chutney, salsa or salad to your plate.

# Duck eggs with fried lettuce, wild herbs and chilli oil

Chunky lettuces, like cos or little gems, are delicious
fried, grilled or roasted and showcase a pan of eggs. In
the spring and early summer I add aromatics like lovage,
sweet cicely leaves, hyssop, marjoram and wild garlic to
the pan before the eggs, but you could also add strips of
smoky bacon. This simple brunch dish is delicious served
with a dollop of garlicky yogurt and Gazpacho salad
(p. 14)

---

**Serves 2**

2 tablespoons olive oil
2–3 garlic cloves, finely chopped
1 cos lettuce or 2 little gems
Juice of ½ a lemon
A handful of lovage leaves
A handful of wild leaves or herbs
4 duck eggs
Sea salt

**For serving:**
½ teaspoon chilli powder
1–2 tablespoons olive oil
6 tablespoons creamy yogurt
1–2 garlic cloves, crushed
Sea salt and freshly ground black pepper

---

Trim the outer leaves of the lettuce and cut off the thick stalk but keep the lettuce intact. If using a cos lettuce, cut it into quarters lengthways; for little gems you can just halve lengthways.

Heat the oil in the frying pan and stir in the garlic. When it begins to go brown, sear the lettuce chunks, turning them over so that the outer leaves take on a bit of colour. Squeeze the lemon juice over them and push them to the sides of the pan.

Toss the lovage and any wild leaves or herbs in the juices in the middle of the pan and make room for the duck eggs. Crack each one into the middle, cover the pan with a lid or aluminium foil and cook over a gentle heat until the whites are firm but the yolks are still runny.

Combine the chilli powder with the olive oil. Quickly beat the yogurt with the garlic in a bowl and season with salt and pepper.

Sprinkle a little sea salt over the eggs, drizzle with chilli oil and serve the lettuce and eggs with dollops of the yogurt and gazpacho salad.

# Wild garlic shakshuka with yogurt

The word 'shakshuka' refers to a dish with eggs cracked into it and there are many variations on the theme served at any time of the day in the Middle East, but in cities like Edinburgh and Glasgow the dish has become trendy to serve for brunch. This recipe is for the classic version, but you can add in ingredients like Great Glen chorizo, fresh prawns, cooked lentils or parboiled potatoes. If it's not wild garlic season, you can replace it with coriander in the ragoût and with sage or thyme in the butter.

---

**Serves 3–4**

2 tablespoons olive oil with a knob of butter
1–2 teaspoons cumin seeds
2 garlic cloves, finely chopped
2 onions, finely sliced
2 bell peppers, finely sliced
1–2 teaspoons honey
1–2 teaspoons dried chilli flakes
2 x 400g (14oz) tins of chopped tomatoes
Sea salt and freshly ground black pepper
A bunch of fresh parsley, finely chopped
A bunch of fresh wild garlic leaves, coarsely chopped
6–8 eggs, depending on the size of your pan and the number
    of people waiting for brunch!

**For the yogurt:**
500g (1lb 2oz) full-fat yogurt

1–2 garlic cloves, crushed
Sea salt and freshly ground black pepper

**For the butter:**
60g (2oz) butter
A handful of wild garlic leaves, finely sliced

---

Heat the oil with the butter in a wide, heavy-based pan.
Stir in the cumin seeds and garlic, until fragrant. Add the
onions and peppers and fry for 3–4 minutes, until they
soften, then stir in the honey, chilli flakes and tomatoes.
Cook gently for about 10 minutes until the mixture
resembles a ragoût.

Meanwhile beat the yogurt with the garlic and
season well. Put aside.

Stir in half the parsley and half the wild garlic and
form pockets in the mixture with the back of a wooden
spoon. Crack the eggs into the pockets, cover the pan
with a lid or a sheet of aluminium foil, and cook gently
until the whites are firm but the yolk is still runny.

Quickly melt the butter in a small pan and, as it
bubbles, stir in the rest of the wild garlic.

Scatter the remaining parsley over the eggs and,
using a spatula, lift each portion out of the pan onto
plates. Spoon a generous dollop of yogurt on top of each
portion and drizzle the butter over the top. Serve with
chunks of crusty bread to mop up all the spicy, buttery,
garlicky flavours.

# Brunch on Bread

# Hot croissants with bacon, Cheddar, avocado and mayonnaise

This simple, satisfying brunch can be made with croissants or toasted rolls and baguettes. For the cheese, we have a variety of delicious tangy Cheddars produced in places like Mull, Lockerbie and Orkney, but you can use any Cheddar you like, or replace it with another firm cheese of your choice. And you can use slices of prosciutto or a baked ham instead of bacon.

**Serves 2**

Olive or rapeseed oil
6–8 rashers of streaky bacon
Butter for spreading
2 large croissants
4 tablespoons grated Cheddar
1 large, ripe avocado, lightly mashed
Mayonnaise for spreading
Freshly ground black pepper

Preheat oven to 180°C (160°C fan), 350°F, Gas 4.

Trickle a little oil into a pan and fry the bacon for a few minutes on each side until golden and crispy.

Slice the croissants in half from end to end and place the base of each one on a baking tray. Spread a little mayonnaise over each one and layer the bacon, cheese and avocado on top. Finish with a good grinding of black pepper and the other croissant half.

Apply a little pressure to bed everything down and then pop the filled croissant into the oven for 10–15 minutes, until the cheese melts and the croissant is lightly toasted.

# Cheesy French toast with garlicky rosemary mushrooms

French toast, or 'eggy bread' as some people refer to it, is a useful brunch base for a variety of roasted or fried ingredients, such as mixed mushrooms – cultivated or wild. For the cheese, choose a semi-hard one that melts easily such as the Highland Fat Cow, Applewood Smoked, Emmental or Gruyère, or opt for slices of Brie or a soft blue cheese.

---

**Serves 2**

**For the French toast:**
2 large eggs
2 tablespoons milk
Sea salt
Freshly ground black pepper
2 slices of white or brown bread
A generous knob of butter
½ tablespoon of sunflower or rapeseed oil
2 tablespoons grated cheese

**For the mushrooms:**
1–2 tablespoons olive or rapeseed oil
1–2 cloves of garlic, finely chopped
1 sprig of rosemary, finely chopped
A few fresh sage leaves

250g (9oz) chestnut mushrooms, mixed mushrooms, or wild
    mushrooms, sliced if large, but kept whole if small
Sea salt
Freshly ground black pepper

---

Beat the eggs in a shallow bowl with the milk. Season
with the salt and pepper and place the slices of bread in
the mixture. Leave to soak.

Heat the oil in a frying pan and toss in the garlic. Just
as it begins to colour, add the rosemary and sage leaves
and toss in the mushrooms. Fry over a high heat until
lightly browned and the pan is almost dry. Season with
salt and pepper and keep warm.

Meanwhile, heat the knob of butter with oil in a
separate pan until it begins to foam. Add the slices of
soaked bread to the pan, pour over any of the egg
mixture left in the bowl, and fry for 2–3 minutes until
golden brown. Flip over the bread slices and scatter the
cheese over the cooked side. Cover with a lid, or a sheet
of aluminium foil, and cook for 2–3 minutes, until the
base of the bread is golden brown and the cheese on top
has melted a little.

Lift the cheesy French toasts out of the pan onto
plates and spoon the mushrooms on top. Serve with
pickles or a salad, such as Gazpacho salad (p. 14),
Guacamole salsa (p. 13) or Tartare potatoes (p. 16).

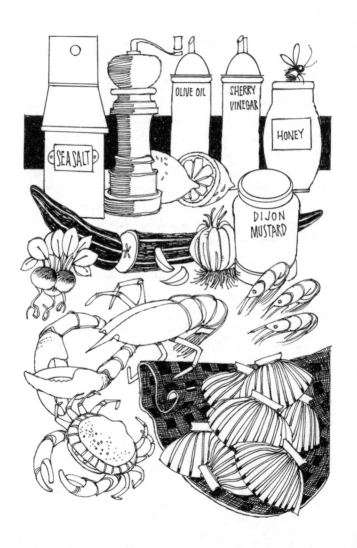

# Pancetta scallops with Caesar salad bruschetta

This brunch take on the classic Caesar salad can be adapted and assembled in any way you like using ingredients like grilled prawns, crabmeat, lobster and eggs. And you could serve a dollop of Garlic mayonnaise (p. 18), Marie Rose sauce (p. 19) or Avocado cream (p. 20) as a creamy accompaniment to the salad.

---

**Serves 2**

**For the dressing:**
3 tablespoons olive oil
1 tablespoon white wine or sherry vinegar
Zest and juice of 1 lemon
1 teaspoon Dijon mustard
1 teaspoon honey
2 teaspoons finely grated Parmesan
Salt and freshly ground black pepper

½ a cucumber
Sea salt
8 fresh scallops, shelled, rinsed and patted dry
8 pancetta rashers
1 small baguette, halved lengthways
Olive oil
1 plump garlic clove, halved
1 gem lettuce, trimmed and shredded
3–4 radishes, finely sliced

A handful fresh broad, or edamame, beans, shelled and cooked
Fresh basil leaves
100g (3½oz) block of Parmesan

---

First make the dressing. Combine all the ingredients in a bowl and whisk until smooth.

For the cucumber ribbons, use a vegetable peeler to cut long, thin strips. Place them in a colander and sprinkle with salt. Leave to weep for 5 minutes, then rinse and pat dry.

Make sure the scallops are patted dry with kitchen paper and wrap a pancetta rasher around the side of each one – press it gently to ensure the bacon remains in place. Heat a non-stick frying pan and drop in a little olive oil. Add the scallops to the pan and fry for about 1 minute on each side so that they turn golden, then roll them around the pan on their sides so the pancetta goes a little crispy. Drain on kitchen paper.

Brush the baguette halves with olive oil and lightly toast them on both sides under the grill or in a griddle pan. Rub them with the garlic halves and then assemble the lettuce, cucumber ribbons, radishes, broad beans and basil leaves on top and place the scallops where you can. Drizzle with the dressing and then, using a vegetable peeler, shave the Parmesan over the top. Serve with mayonnaise or one of the suggested creamy sauces.

# Orkney marinated herring with granola Waldorf salad on rye bread

I'm cheating a little with this brunch as I'm using a shop-bought tub of marinated herring. Why? Because the Orkney herring is so good! Quick and easy to assemble, this light brunch is Scandinavian in style, but you can swap the rye bread for one of your own choice.

---

**Serves 2**

**For the salad:**
1 apple, cut into long, thin strips
Juice of ½ a lemon
2 celery stalks, trimmed and thinly sliced
6 ready-to-eat dried apricots, thinly sliced
1 tablespoon sultanas
1 tablespoon pumpkin seeds
1 tablespoon sunflower seeds

**For the dressing:**
2 tablespoons mayonnaise
2 tablespoons Greek yogurt
Zest and juice of 1 lemon
Sea salt and freshly ground black pepper

1 x 400g (14oz) tub of Orkney sweet marinated herring in dill, or one of the other marinades in the Orkney selection
4 slices toasted rye bread, pumpernickel, or a bread of your choice

Butter, for spreading
1 teaspoon linseeds
1 tablespoon porridge oats, toasted

---

Tip the apple into a bowl and toss it in the lemon juice. Add the rest of the salad ingredients to the bowl. Beat the dressing ingredients together and add enough to just coat the salad.

Drain the herring and cut into bite-sized pieces. Toast the slices of rye bread, spread them with butter, and arrange the herring and salad on top, alternating in a haphazard fashion.

Spoon any leftover dressing on top, sprinkle the linseeds over everything and finish with the toasted oats.

Baked Potato Brunch

Parsley

Chives

Sorrel

Wild Garlic

Thyme

Sage

The humble potato has long been a staple in the Scottish diet, but I don't know why we don't see more baked potato combinations for brunch as they are brilliant for packing with salads and pâtés, scrambled eggs and spicy beans, smoked fish, grilled bacon or sautéed mushrooms, topped with sauces, soured cream, grated or melted cheese, pickles, herbs and chillies, even a fried or poached egg. They represent an 'anything goes' type of brunch, and they will certainly fill your belly for a day in the hills or a long journey ahead.

To me the perfect baked potatoes should be crispy-skinned with a crunch of salt, and for that extra dash of flavour a little bit of butter should melt in the cushion of steaming flesh before piling on the filling.

To flavour the butter, leave it out of the fridge to soften, then beat it in a bowl with aromatic seasonings such as chopped wild garlic, chives, sorrel, parsley, thyme, sage or mint, or crushed garlic, chillies, cumin, allspice, black pepper, seaweed, preserved lemon or orange zest.

For the crispy-skinned baked potato, I prick mine all over with a fork, rub each one with olive or rapeseed oil and then grind a generous amount of salt and black pepper over them. I bake them in a hot oven for anything from 1 to 2 hours, depending on the size of the potato, until they are crispy on the outside but give to the press of a finger.

In our family, we call these 'Rock 'n' Roll Potatoes' as that is exactly what they are designed to do!

# Baked potato with smoked salmon and chilli scrambled eggs

Chilli scrambled eggs work well with smoked salmon and Blood Mary salad (p. 12) – perhaps an actual Bloody Mary too. You can prepare the scrambled eggs with fresh herbs, such as dill and parsley, if you don't like chilli.

---

**Serves 2**

**For the potatoes:**
2 good-sized crispy-skinned baked potatoes, freshly baked, hot and
     ready to rock and roll
Salted butter, flavoured with parsley

**For the scrambled eggs:**
6–8 eggs
Sea salt and freshly ground black pepper
1 tablespoon butter or olive oil
1–2 fresh red or green chillies, deseeded and finely chopped
1 red onion, finely chopped
1 large tomato, deseeded and finely chopped
1 teaspoon ground turmeric
Fresh coriander, finely chopped
2 slices smoked salmon, cut into thin strips

**For serving:**
4 generous slices of smoked salmon
Lemon wedges for squeezing

Freshly ground black pepper
A small bunch fresh parsley, finely chopped
Ketchup, chilli sauce or chutney

_____

Beat the eggs lightly with a fork in a bowl and season
with salt and pepper.

Melt the butter in a heavy-based pan and stir in the
chillies and onion for 2 minutes, add the chopped
tomatoes and stir in the turmeric and most of the
coriander. Tip in the eggs and the strips of salmon and
stir gently one way and then the other a few times until
they begin to scramble.

Place the hot baked potatoes on plates, split open
with a knife, score the flesh and slip in the butter to melt.
Spoon the scrambled egg onto the baked potato and
arrange the salmon slices with lemon wedges on the
plate. Garnish with the parsley and serve with the Bloody
Mary salad and any sauce or chutney of your choice.

# Baked potato with lemon lovage tuna salad

Everyone is familiar with a baked potato filled with tuna salad but it is usually served for lunch or supper and so often it misses the mark – the tuna is too dry or sloppy depending on the quantity of cheap mayo, the potato too heavy and soft as it has been pre-cooked and microwaved – yet if you put a little love into it and get it right, it is a great combo and makes a cheap, hearty and satisfying brunch to which you could add soft-boiled eggs on the side, or a fried egg on top. If you can't get lovage, you could substitute the flavour with celery leaves and add a few celery sticks to the plate.

---

**Serves 2**

**For the potatoes:**
2 crispy-skinned baked potatoes, freshly baked, hot and ready to rock and roll
Salted butter, flavoured with wild garlic or chives, if possible

**For the tuna:**
3 x 145g (5¼oz) tins of tuna in brine, rinsed and drained
1 red onion, finely chopped
Zest and juice of 1 lemon
4 tablespoons thick, creamy mayonnaise
A fistful of fresh chives, chopped

A handful of wild garlic leaves, chopped
A handful of lovage, or celery, leaves, shredded
Sea salt and freshly ground black pepper

---

Keep the baked potatoes warm while you prepare the tuna. Tip the drained canned fish into a bowl. Add all the other ingredients, mix well, and season to taste with salt and pepper.

Split open the potatoes and place them on plates. Slip in the wild garlic butter to melt and spoon the tuna salad on top. Serve with halved soft-boiled eggs, if you like.

# Baked potato with haggis and marmalade chipolatas

To some observers, my father had some peculiar culinary indulgences and one of them was his enjoyment of sausages with marmalade. If they weren't baked in it, like honey sausages, then he would simply dip his cooked sausage into a little marmalade like someone else might do with mustard. He was not alone in this as I have encountered several other Scots of my generation and older who do the same – perhaps it's a Scottish 'thing' – and, to be honest, if you combine good-quality pork chipolatas with Seville orange marmalade, it is really good. Add some subtly spiced haggis from your local butcher and you've got yourself a brunch fit for a hardy Highlander and, if you top it with a fried egg, you'll be ready to toss the caber at the local Games!

---

**Serves 2**

**For the potatoes:**
2 good-sized crispy-skinned baked potatoes, freshly baked,
     hot and ready to rock and roll
Salted butter

1 x small cooked haggis, or leftover haggis
Roughly 12 chipolatas

A drizzle of sunflower oil
2 tablespoons Seville orange marmalade

---

Preheat the oven to 200°C (180°C fan), 400°F, Gas 6.

If you are cooking the haggis first, simmer it in its skin according to the instructions (roughly 40 minutes). Place the haggis on a piece of foil, slit it open and pull up the sides of the foil, leaving the slit exposed. Pop the haggis in the oven for 15–20 minutes.

Place the chipolatas in an ovenproof dish, drizzle with the sunflower oil and pop them in the oven for 20 minutes. Add the marmalade, lightly coating the sausages, and pop them back into the oven for another 10–15 minutes, until they are brown and sticky.

Take the potatoes out of the oven, split them open and scoop the flesh into a bowl. Add a generous knob of butter to melt over the flesh and scoop most of the haggis into the bowl. Carefully fold the potato and haggis together, but don't mash them into a mush. Pile the mixture back into potatoes and spoon the rest of the haggis on top.

Pile the marmalade sausages over and around the potatoes and drizzle with some of the juices from the dish. Serve hot with a fried egg or a salad, if you like.

# Baked potato with curry beans and smoked cheese

Baked potatoes, tinned baked beans and Cheddar cheese form another Scottish belly-filler. It's quick and easy and, for some, it's comfort food, so why not spice up the beans for a brunch topped with a smoked cheese, such as Applewood Smoked, and served with soured cream and Guacamole salsa (p. 13), or with Avocado cream (p. 20).

---

**Serves 2**

**For the potatoes:**
2 good-sized crispy-skinned baked potatoes, freshly baked, hot and ready to rock and roll
Salted butter, flavoured with crushed garlic

**For the beans:**
1 tablespoon rapeseed oil
1 teaspoon cumin seeds
2 garlic cloves, finely chopped
A finger-sized piece of ginger, peeled and finely chopped
1 onion, chopped
2 x 400g (14oz) cans of mixed or cannellini beans, drained and rinsed
1 teaspoon dried chilli flakes
1–2 teaspoons curry powder
1 tablespoon tomato paste
Juice of 1 lemon
1–2 teaspoons honey

A small bunch fresh coriander, finely chopped
Sea salt
150g (5oz) smoked firm cheese, grated

**For serving:**
Soured cream
Guacamole salsa

---

Heat the oil in a pan and stir in the cumin seeds for a minute. Stir in the garlic, ginger and onion until they begin to colour, then toss in the beans, coating them in the onion mixture. Add the chilli flakes, curry powder, tomato paste, lemon juice and honey and mix well – add a little water if your pan is too dry – and cook gently for 5–10 minutes. Toss in half the coriander and season well to taste.

Slit open the potatoes, score the flesh and slip in the garlic-flavoured butter to melt. Pile on most of the beans and scatter the cheese over the top. Place the potatoes back in the oven, or under the grill to melt the cheese. Garnish with the rest of the coriander and serve with soured cream, guacamole salsa or avocado cream.

CORIANDER

Sweet Tooth Brunch

# Granola

Homemade granola is handy for brunch. Even if you don't feel like preparing anything, you can sprinkle it over shop-bought or leftover labneh, yogurt, rice pudding, mashed bananas, stewed or fresh fruits, or use it as crumble topping. The great thing about making your own is that you can make it as spicy as you like and choose your dried fruits. Use this recipe as a guide for your own concoction and store in an airtight container for 2–3 weeks – if it lasts that long!

---

**Makes enough for about 8 portions**

125ml (4½fl oz) vegetable oil
200ml (7fl oz) maple syrup
250g (9oz) porridge oats
85g (3oz) pumpkin seeds
85g (3oz) sunflower seeds
85g (3oz) linseeds
85g (3oz) poppy seeds
85g (3oz) sesame seeds
150g (5oz) flaked almonds
150g (5oz) desiccated coconut
1 tablespoon ground cinnamon
1 teaspoon grated nutmeg
1 teaspoon ground turmeric
250g (9oz) dried fruit – e.g. sultanas, raisins, cranberries, blueberries
    or chopped apricots, dates, prunes

---

Preheat the oven to 150°C (130°C fan), 300°F, Gas 2.

In a bowl, whisk the oil with the maple syrup. Place all the other ingredients in a separate bowl and mix well. Pour in the oil and maple syrup and stir well to make sure everything is coated in it. Tip the mixture onto a baking tray, spread it out evenly and pop it in the oven for about 15 minutes.

Rake through the granola with a fork to break up lumps and prevent the edges from cooking too quickly and return to the oven for a further 15 minutes, or until it is golden and smelling delicious! Rake it one more time, leave to cool and store.

# Cranachan smoothie

Brunch doesn't always have to be a cooked affair. Sometimes you might just want something simple, healthy and nourishing and this smoothie take on the traditional Scottish pudding, cranachan, might be all you need. You can make this blend of fresh raspberries and oatmeal as thick as porridge and top it with a dollop of yogurt and more raspberries, blueberries, or blackcurrants, or you can thin it with yogurt and drink it alongside your main brunch dish. Feel free to add a splash of whisky to it too – you might as well get into the spirit of a cheerful brunch!

**Serves 2–4**

115g (4oz) medium or pinhead oatmeal
Milk
500g (1lb 2oz) fresh raspberries (reserve a few for the top)
1 tablespoon honey
3–4 tablespoons creamy yogurt

In order to enjoy this smoothie for brunch you need to start preparing it the night before. Tip the oatmeal into a bowl and pour in enough milk to just cover the grains and leave to soak overnight.

In the morning, scrape the soaked oatmeal into a blender with the raspberries and whisk to a thick, smooth puree. Add the honey to taste – if the raspberries are in season they are usually quite sweet so you won't need much – and add the yogurt. Blend again and adjust the consistency to suit your palate and your mood by adding more yogurt, or a little water.

Tip the smoothie into bowls, or pour it into glasses, and top it with the reserved raspberries. Enjoy it chilled or at room temperature.

# Bread and butter pudding

I don't often eat a pudding at the end of an evening meal but if it's there in the fridge, I really enjoy leftover apple tart, fruit crumble, or bread pudding for brunch. Served hot or cold, this light bread and butter pudding is delicious with poached rhubarb, with fresh summer berries or, how my granny used to like it, with hot raspberry jam.

---

**Serves 4**

300ml (10fl oz) milk
300ml (10fl oz) single cream
1 vanilla pod, split open
A pinch of salt
4 eggs
115g (4oz) caster sugar or vanilla sugar
50g (2oz) butter, at room temperature
5–6 thin slices of white bread or brioche
2 tablespoons sultanas
Icing sugar, for dusting

---

Heat the milk and cream in a saucepan with the vanilla pod and salt until scalding hot – don't boil – then turn off the heat, cover and leave to infuse for about 30 minutes. Lift the vanilla pod out of the milk and squeeze the seeds back in for flavour.

In a bowl, whisk the eggs and sugar together and,

gradually, whisk in the infused milk and cream.

Choose a shallow baking dish with a volume capacity for 1.2 litres (2 pints) and rub a little of the butter around the edges and over the base. Butter the slices of bread, cut them in half diagonally, and arrange them around the dish so that the crusts are over the rim. Scatter the sultanas over the bread then carefully pour the milk and egg mixture down the sides of the dish. Leave the bread to soak for about 2 hours.

Preheat the oven to 160°C (140°C fan), 325°F, Gas 3. Place the dish in a bain-marie and bake for 35–40 minutes, until just firm to touch. Dust the top with icing sugar and pop the pudding under a hot grill for a few seconds to lightly caramelize. Serve hot or cold with fresh blackcurrants, raspberries or strawberries.

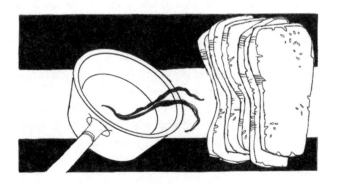

# Baked oat and apple pudding, crowdie and strawberries

Quick and easy, this is more like a large baked muffin than a pudding and can be paired with any seasonal fruits, jams, or syrups, and finished with whipped cream or crowdie, which is a traditional Scottish curd cheese.

**Serves 4**

120ml (4fl oz) sunflower oil
2 eggs, beaten
175g (6oz) soft brown sugar
300g (10oz) porridge oats
1–2 teaspoons ground ginger

2 teaspoons baking powder
1 teaspoon salt
2 apples, peeled, cored and grated
250ml (9fl oz) milk

**For serving:**
4 tablespoons crowdie or whipped cream
Fresh strawberries, or fruit of your choice

Preheat the oven to 180°C (160°C fan), 350°F, Gas 4. Whisk the oil with the eggs and sugar in a wide bowl. Stir in the oats, ginger, baking powder and salt, add the grated apple and pour in the milk. Mix well.

Lightly grease an ovenproof dish, approximately 20cm (8in) in diameter, and tip in the mixture. Pop the dish into the oven for 35–40 minutes until golden and firm to touch. Serve hot with fresh strawberries and crowdie or cream.

# Banana and cinnamon fritters with smoked bacon and raspberries with lime

These banana fritters from my childhood are delicious on their own as a sweet snack or for brunch with smoked bacon and fruit. If you like Canadian pancakes with maple syrup and bacon, you will love these.

---

**Serves 4**

**For the fritters:**
4 tablespoons rice flour
4–6 ripe bananas
1–2 teaspoons ground cinnamon
1 tablespoon soft brown or coconut sugar
1 egg
Sunflower oil

8–12 rashers of streaky bacon
200g (7oz) fresh raspberries
Juice and zest of 1 fresh lime
Icing sugar, for dusting

---

First toast the rice flour. You can either do this in a skillet over the stove, or by roasting it on a baking tray in the oven. You just want it to begin to go brown.

Mash the bananas with a fork in a bowl – not too smooth as it's nice to have some lumpy bits. Beat in the cinnamon and sugar. Beat in the toasted rice flour while it's still warm and then beat in the egg.

Heat enough oil in a wok or deep pan for frying and drop in spoonfuls of the banana mixture. Cook in batches for less than a minute until firm and golden on both sides. Drain on kitchen paper and keep warm.

Grill or pan-fry the bacon until crispy and arrange on plates with the fritters and a handful of raspberries. Squeeze the lime over the raspberries and sprinkle with the zest. Dust everything with the icing sugar and serve while still warm.

# French toast bacon butties with honey gooseberries

Added to our reputation for deep-frying everything, we Scots are also known for our butties – with chips, potato crisps, sausage, and bacon. Here the bacon butties are finished with gooseberries in honey syrup in the tradition of Canada's pancakes, topped with bacon and maple syrup.

---

**Serves 2**

**For the gooseberries:**
200g (7oz) gooseberries, topped and tailed
4 tablespoons honey

**For the butties:**
2 eggs
180ml (6fl oz) milk
1 tablespoon granulated sugar
4 slices white or brown bread, cut in half on the diagonal
8 rashers streaky bacon, grilled
2 tablespoons butter

**For serving:**
Icing sugar

---

First prepare the gooseberries. Tip the gooseberries into a heatproof bowl with the honey. Cover the bowl with cling film and set over a pan of simmering water for about 30 minutes until the fruit is soft but still holds its shape. Take the bowl off the pan, strain the juice into a small saucepan and bring it to the boil. Reduce the heat and bubble gently until the juice has reduced to a thick syrup. Pour the syrup over the gooseberries and leave to cool.

Whisk the eggs and milk with the sugar in a bowl. Place the diagonally-halved bread in the egg/milk mixture. Leave to soak.

Place the bacon rashers under the grill, or fry them in a pan, until golden and crisp. Keep warm in aluminium foil.

Heat 1 tablespoon of the butter in a non-stick frying pan and fry two slices of the soaked bread for about 3 minutes each side until golden and crisp. Keep warm and repeat with the rest.

Place the bacon between two triangles of the fried bread to make a sandwich – you should end up with four butties – and spoon the gooseberries and honey syrup over them. Dust with icing sugar and enjoy while they're still hot.

# Fluffy ricotta pancakes with roasted rose rhubarb, yogurt and granola

Drop scones and pancakes are always an easy choice for brunch and you can play around with the mix, by using buttermilk or coconut milk instead of regular full-fat milk, and different flours, such as wholemeal or buckwheat. You can't go wrong by topping them with stewed or fresh fruit, yogurt, crème fraîche or cream and a dusting of toasted oats or Granola (p. 72).

---

**Serves 4**

4 rhubarb stalks, cut into bite-sized pieces
1 tablespoon butter
1 teaspoon vanilla extract
2 tablespoons granulated sugar
1 tablespoon rose water

**For the pancakes:**
175g (6oz) ricotta
100ml (3½fl oz) milk
2 large eggs, separated
100g (3½ oz) plain flour
1 teaspoon baking powder
Pinch of salt
Butter

**For serving:**
4 tablespoons Greek yogurt, crème fraîche or whipped cream
Rose petal or raspberry jam
Granola

---

Heat the oven to 180°C (160°C fan), 350°F, Gas 4.

Place the rhubarb in an ovenproof dish. Melt the butter in a small pan, stir in the vanilla extract and sugar and pour over the rhubarb. Pop the dish in the oven for about 15 minutes, until the rhubarb is tender but not mush. Splash the rosewater over the rhubarb and leave to cool.

To make the pancakes, whisk the ricotta with the milk and egg yolks in a bowl. Gradually sift in the flour with the baking powder and salt, whisking all the time. In a separate bowl, whisk the egg whites until stiff and then gradually fold them into the pancake mixture.

Heat a little butter in a non-stick frying pan. Cook large spoonfuls of the pancake batter in batches until golden on both sides. Keep warm until you have finished all the pancakes.

Assemble the pancakes on plates. Spoon the rhubarb on top, followed by a spoon of yogurt, a dollop of jam, and a sprinkling of granola.

# Hot scones with grilled plums and crowdie

Everyone loves a scone – plain, fruit or savoury – and some people are very particular about the size and texture of theirs. I prefer a plain hot scone and then add the savoury or the sweet to it, such as sweet plums or jam with crowdie, tart yogurt or labneh, cream cheese or crème fraîche.

---

**Serves 4**

225g (8oz) self-raising flour
A pinch of salt
40g (1½oz) golden caster sugar
40g (1½oz) butter, chilled and diced
1 egg
125ml (4floz) milk

**For the plums:**
4 ripe plums, halved and stoned
1 teaspoon vanilla bean paste
6 tablespoons mascarpone
3 tablespoons soft brown sugar

**For serving:**
Crowdie, clotted cream, whipped butter, or cream cheese

---

Preheat the oven to 220°C (200°C fan), 425°F, Gas 7.

Sift the flour and salt into a bowl and mix in the sugar. Rub the butter into the flour, using your fingertips, until it resembles fine breadcrumbs. Lightly beat the egg with the milk, pour it into the flour and use a round-bladed knife to combine it. Knead into soft dough.

Turn the dough onto a floured surface and knead into a soft ball. Roll the dough out and use pastry cutters or an up-turned glass or cup to cut out 8 scones or more, depending on the size of the cutter.

Arrange the rounds of dough on a lightly greased baking tray – make sure you leave a little space between them as they will expand on cooking – and pop them in the oven for 12–15 minutes, until firm and golden brown.

While the scones are baking, prepare the plums. Place them in an ovenproof dish skin-side down. Combine the mascarpone with the vanilla paste and spoon it over the plums. Sprinkle the brown sugar over the top and place the plums under the grill to caramelize.

Serve the scones hot with the grilled plums and enjoy them with crowdie or a topping of your own choice.

# Summer berry slump with dumplings, yogurt and granola

Adapted from a traditional German pudding, this is such an easy way to prepare fresh or frozen berries for a satisfying brunch. I pick the blackcurrants, redcurrants and gooseberries in my garden and the wild raspberries on my walks in the countryside, and then freeze some of them in mixed batches for crumbles and sauces and this brunch slump. You can replace the creamy yogurt with coconut yogurt, whipped cream or crème fraîche.

**Serves 3–4**

500g (1lb 2oz) fresh or frozen mixed berries
4 tablespoons granulated sugar
2 tablespoons gin, or water

60g (2oz) self-raising flour
30g (1oz) butter, chilled and diced
2 teaspoons caster sugar
1 teaspoon grated orange or tangerine zest
1 teaspoon cinnamon
2 tablespoons milk

**For serving:**
3–4 tablespoons Granola (p. 72)
3–4 tablespoons thick, creamy yogurt

Preheat the oven to 190°C (170°C fan), 375°F, Gas 5.

Put the fresh or frozen fruit into a baking dish, sprinkle with the sugar and add the water or gin. Cover with aluminium foil and bake in the oven for about 10 minutes, until the juices begin to run.

Meanwhile, sift the flour into a bowl and rub in the butter until the mixture resembles fine breadcrumbs. Stir in the sugar, cinnamon and orange zest and bind with the milk to form a soft dough. Take small portions of the dough and roll it into balls.

Gently stir the fruit in the baking dish and place the dumplings in the juices. Cover with foil and return the dish to the oven for about 15 minutes, until the dumplings are firm to touch. Serve the slump straight from the dish, or spoon it into individual bowls with dollops of thick, creamy yogurt and granola sprinkled over the top.

# Boozy Brunch

Just as there are no rules for brunch, there are none for the drinks to go with it. A variety of hot and chilled coffees and teas or pressed fruit and vegetable juices and smoothies are all good companions, but when special occasions call for booze, it is often a bit of fizz that sits at the top of the list. So, here are a variety of cocktail suggestions that might suit the occasion.

# Mimosa

If you omit the Grand Marnier and measure one-third orange juice to two-thirds champagne you have a classic Buck's Fizz, or one-third peach juice to two-thirds prosecco to make a Bellini.

---

**Serves 4–6**

---

2–3 fresh oranges, squeezed
4–6 teaspoons Grand Marnier (optional)
1 bottle champagne or prosecco, chilled

---

Pour the orange juice into well-chilled champagne flutes to fill them by one-quarter. Add the Grand Marnier, if using, and top off with the chilled champagne. Lightly stir and serve.

# Whisky Highball

---

**Serves 2**

60ml (2fl oz) Scotch whisky of your choice
120–150ml (4–5fl oz) sparkling water
Strips of lemon zest
2–3 mint leaves
Ice

---

Fill two glasses with ice. Pour in the whisky and add the
water. Drop in the lemon zest and garnish with the mint.

# Whisky Sour

**Serves 2**

120ml (4fl oz) Scotch whisky
Juice of 1 lemon
2 teaspoons sugar syrup
Ice cubes
Lemon and lime zest

Put the whisky, lemon juice and sugar syrup into a
cocktail shaker with a handful of ice cubes and shake
vigorously. Strain into two cocktail glasses and garnish
them with strips of lemon and lime zest.

# The Horse's Neck

If you replace the brandy with gin, this cocktail is called
On the Hoof.

**Serves 2**

Angostura bitters
Ice cubes
120ml (4fl oz) brandy
300ml (½ pint) ginger ale
2 lemons

Add a good dash of Angostura to two tall glasses and
swirl them to lightly coat the inside. Half fill each glass
with ice and pour in the brandy, followed by the ginger
ale. Using a sharp knife or potato peeler, cut around each
lemon to remove the zest in a long thin spiral. Hang the
spiral over the sides of each glass, stretching it to the base.

# Bloody Mary

**Serves 2**

A large handful of ice
100ml (3½fl oz) vodka
500ml (17fl oz) tomato juice
1 tablespoon lemon juice
Worcestershire sauce
Tabasco
A pinch celery salt
A pinch black pepper
Slices of lemon, to serve

Place the ice in a large jug. Measure the vodka, tomato juice and lemon juice and pour it straight onto the ice. Add 3 shakes each of Worcestershire sauce and Tabasco, or more to taste, and season with the celery salt and pepper. Stir until the outside of the jug feels cold, then strain the cocktail into 2 tall glasses. Top up with fresh ice and add a lemon slice to each glass.

# Espresso Martini

---

**Serves 2**

100g (3½oz) golden caster sugar
A handful of ice
100ml (3½fl oz) vodka
50ml (4 tablespoons) freshly brewed espresso coffee
50ml (4 tablespoons) coffee liqueur
Coffee beans, for serving (optional)

---

First make the sugar syrup. Put the sugar into a pan with roughly 50ml water and bring it to the boil, stirring all the time. Reduce the heat and simmer for 5 minutes. Turn off the heat and leave the syrup to cool.

Place two cocktail glasses in the fridge to chill. Pour 1 tablespoon of the cooled syrup into a cocktail shaker along with the ice, vodka, espresso and coffee liqueur. Shake until the outside of the shaker feels icy cold.

Strain the cocktail into the chilled glasses and garnish with coffee beans, if you like.

# Hair of the Dog

Just in case your brunch is after a late night of heavy drinking, this might be the boozy option for you!

---

**Serves 2**

120ml (4fl oz) Scotch whisky
90ml (3fl oz) double cream
2 tablespoons honey
Ice cubes or crushed ice

---

Whisk together the whisky, cream and honey in a bowl, or shake them vigorously in a cocktail shaker. Pour into a tumbler over ice.